THE SMITHS

BEST II

Folio © 1992 International Music Publications Limited
Southend Road, Woodford Green, Essex IG8 8HN England
Printed by Panda Press · Haverhill · Suffolk

THE SMITHS BEST II

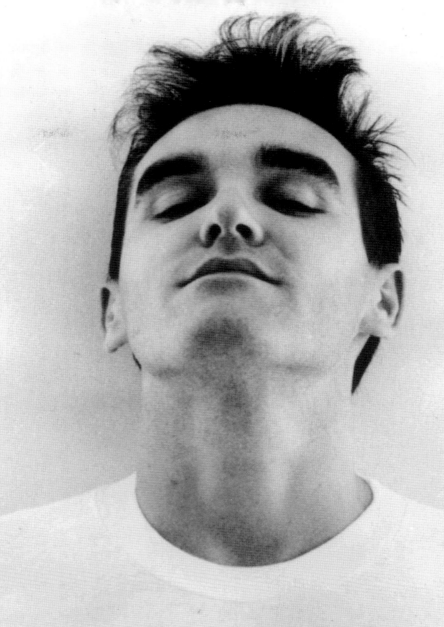

THE BOY WITH THE THORN IN HIS SIDE

Words by MORRISSEY
Music by JOHNNY MARR

lieve me__ now_____ will they ev will they ev - er_____ be-lieve me? Oh_____

(INTRO.)

__ Oh_____ Oh_____ Oh_____

CHORUS: The boy with the thorn in his side
behind the hatred there lies
a plundering desire for love

VERSE 2: How can they see the love in our eyes
and still they don't believe us
and after all this time
they don't want to believe us
and if they don't believe us now
will they ever believe us
and when you want to Live
how do you start?
where do you go?
who do you need to know?

INTRO: (Repeat)

CHORUS: (Instr.)

THE HEADMASTER RITUAL

Words by MORRISSEY
Music by JOHNNY MARR

INSTR: ‖: E / Cmaj7(+9) / E / Cmaj7(+9) / Dmaj7(+9) / Gmaj7 (+9) / Cmaj7 (+9) :‖

INTRO: (Repeat)

VERSE 2: Belligerent ghouls
Run Manchester schools
Spineless bastards all
Sir leads the troops
Jealous of youth
Same old jokes since 1902
He does the military two-step
Down the nape of my neck
I wanna go home
I don't want to stay
Give up life
As a bad mistake
Please excuse me from gym
I've got this terrible cold coming on
He grabs and devours
He kicks me in the showers
Kicks me in the showers
And he grabs and devours
I wanna go home
I don't want to stay.

INSTR: (Repeat) — Fade

HEAVEN KNOWS I'M MISERABLE NOW

Words by MORRISSEY
Music by JOHNNY MARR

peo-ple who don't care if I _____ live or die_____

ASK

Words by MORRISSEY
Music by JOHNNY MARR

21

OSCILLATE WILDLY

Music by
MORRISSEY & JOHNNY MARR

D.S. Repeat ad lib. to Fade

NOWHERE FAST

Words by MORRISSEY
Music by JOHNNY MARR

da da da   da   da da da da da   it's such a___

___ sad   thing. ___

VERSE 2:   I'd like to drop my trousers to the Queen
             Every sensible child will know what this means
             The poor and the needy
             Are selfish and greedy on her terms
             And if the day came when I felt a
             natural emotion
             I'd get such a shock I'd probably jump
             In the ocean
             And when a train goes by
             It's such a sad sound oh. . . .
             It's such a sad thing.

INSTR: F♯m / F♯m   / F♯m   / F♯m   / F♯m / Em / G / A
                          /D   /E   /D

VERSE 3:   And when I'm lying in my bed
             I think about life
             And I think about death
             And neither one particularly appeals to me
             And if the day came when I felt a
             Natural emotion
             I'd get such a shock I'd probably lie
             In the middle of the street and die
             I'd lie down and die.

END: Bm / A / Ĝ

STILL ILL

Words by MORRISSEY
Music by JOHNNY MARR

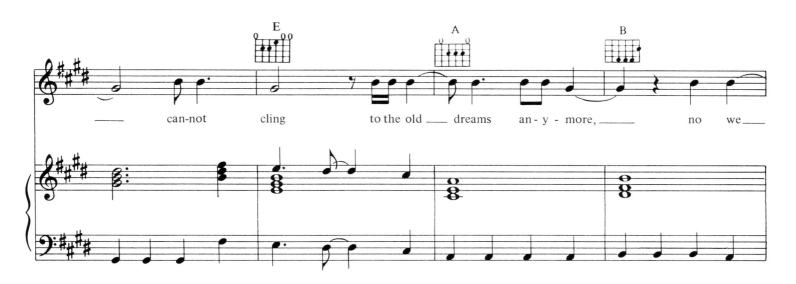

can-not cling to the old ___ dreams an-y-more, ___ no we___

can-not cling ___ to those ___ dreams. ___ (2. Does the)

VERSE 2:   Does the body rule the mind
Or does the mind rule the body?
I dunno. . . .

Under the iron bridge we kissed
And although I ended up with sore lips
It just wasn't like the old days anymore
No, it wasn't like those days
Am I still ill?

VERSE 3:   Does the body rule the mind
Or does the mind rule the body?
I dunno. . . .

Ask me why, and I'll die
Ask me why, and I'll die
And if you must go to work tomorrow
Well, if I were you I wouldn't bother.

VERSE 4:   For there are brighter sides to life
And I should know because I've seen them
But not very often. . . .
Under the iron bridge we kissed
And although I ended up with sore lips
It just wasn't like the old days anymore
No, it wasn't like those days
Am I still ill?

BRIDGE: E / A / B / G♯m / E / A / B
+ Oh am I still ill?

INTRO: *(Repeat) – END on C♯m7*

BIGMOUTH STRIKES AGAIN

Words by MORRISSEY
Music by JOHNNY MARR

nose and her {Walk - man / hear - ing aid} start-ed to___ melt.___

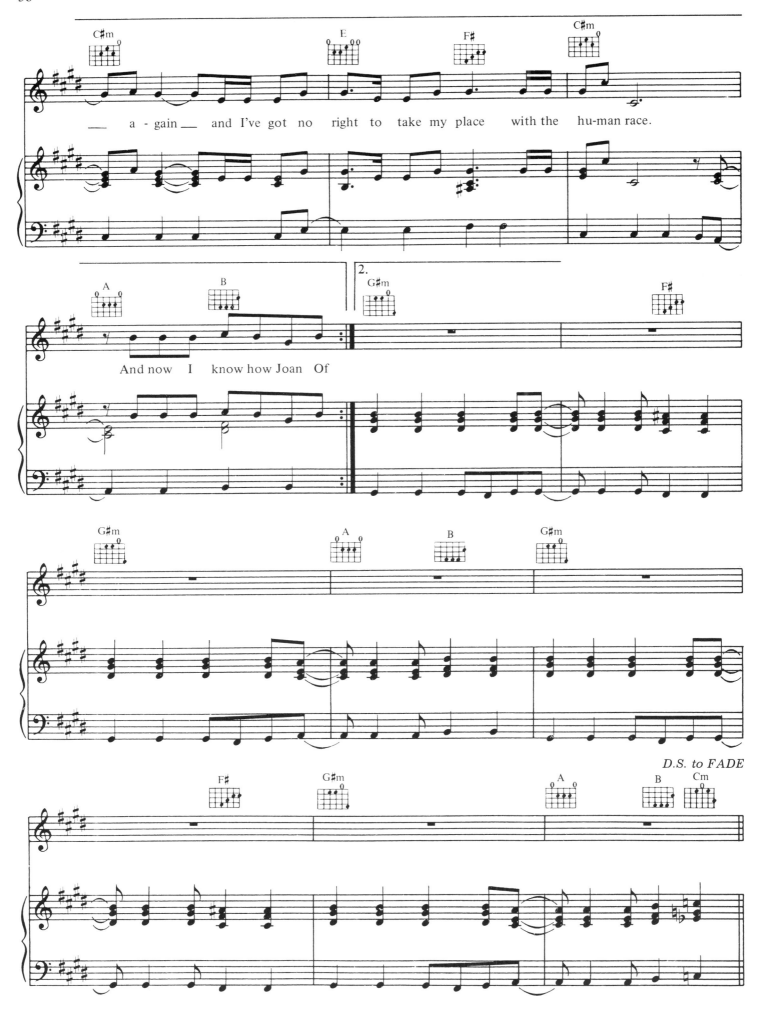

THAT JOKE ISN'T FUNNY ANYMORE

Words by MORRISSEY
Music by JOHNNY MARR

SHAKESPEARE'S SISTER

Words by MORRISSEY
Music by JOHNNY MARR

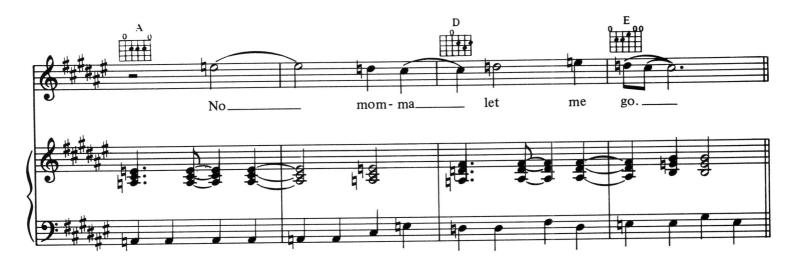

No_____ mom - ma_____ let me go. _____

½ Intro:	(Repeat)
Verse 2:	Young bones groan And the Rocks below say: "Throw your white body down" But I'm going to meet the one I love At last, at last, at last I'm going to meet the one I love La-de-dah-la-de-dah No momma let me go
Instr:	D / G / Em / A / Em / A / D / E / F♯ / A / D / E
½ Intro:	(Repeat)
Verse 3:	I thought that if you had an acoustic guitar Then it meant that you were A protest singer I can smile about it now But at the time it was terrible No momma let me go
Ending:	B / D / E / F♯

GIRL AFRAID

Words by MORRISSEY
Music by JOHNNY MARR

REEL AROUND THE FOUNTAIN

Words by MORRISSEY
Music by JOHNNY MARR

It's time the tale were told ___ of how ___ you took a child ___

___ and ___ you made _____ him old ___

it's time the tale were told ___ of how ___ you took a child ___

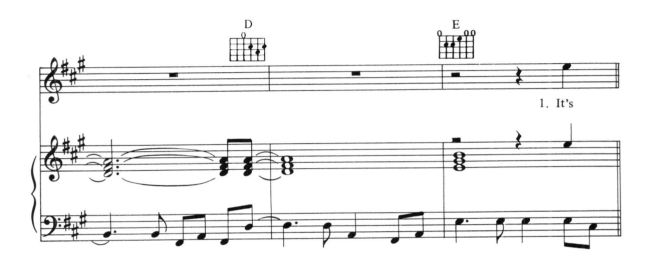

1. It's

VERSE 1 + CHORUS: *(Repeat)*

MIDDLE: Fifteen minutes with you
Oh I wouldn't say no
People see no worth in you
Oh but I do

VERSE 2: I dreamt about you last night
And I fell out of bed twice
You can pin and mount me like a butterfly
But take me to the haven of your bed
Was something that you never said
Two lumps, please
You're the bee's knees
But so am I.

CHORUS: Meet me at the fountain
Shove me on the patio
I'll take it slowly.

MIDDLE: *(Repeat as 2º)*

LAST NIGHT I DREAMT THAT SOMEBODY LOVED ME

Words by MORRISSEY
Music by JOHNNY MARR

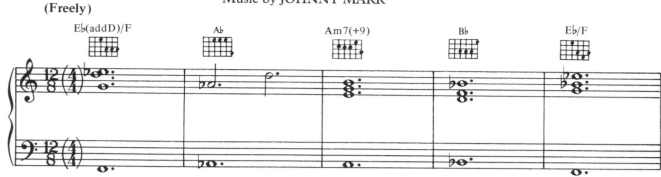

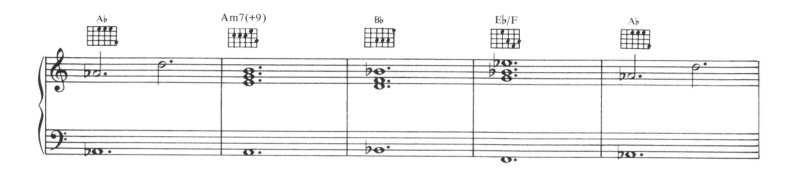

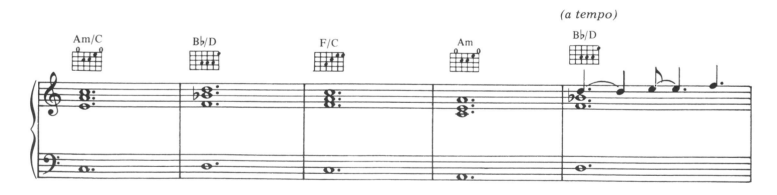

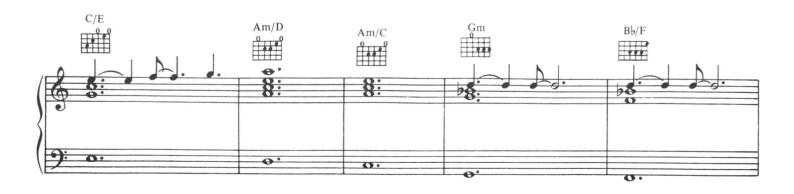

THERE IS A LIGHT THAT NEVER GOES OUT

Words by MORRISSEY
Music by JOHNNY MARR

VERSE 2:
Take me out tonight
Because I want to see people and I
Want to see lights
Driving in your car
Oh please don't drop me home
Because, it's not my home, it's their
home, and I'm welcome no more.

VERSE 3:
Take me out tonight
Oh take me anywhere, I don't care
And in the darkened underpass
I thought, oh God, my chance has come at last
(But then a strange fear gripped me and I
Just couldn't ask).

VERSE 4:
Take me out tonight
Take me anywhere, I don't care
Just drive in your car
I never never want to go home
Because I haven't got one
I haven't got one.

Printed in England
Panda Press · Haverhill · Suffolk • 2/93